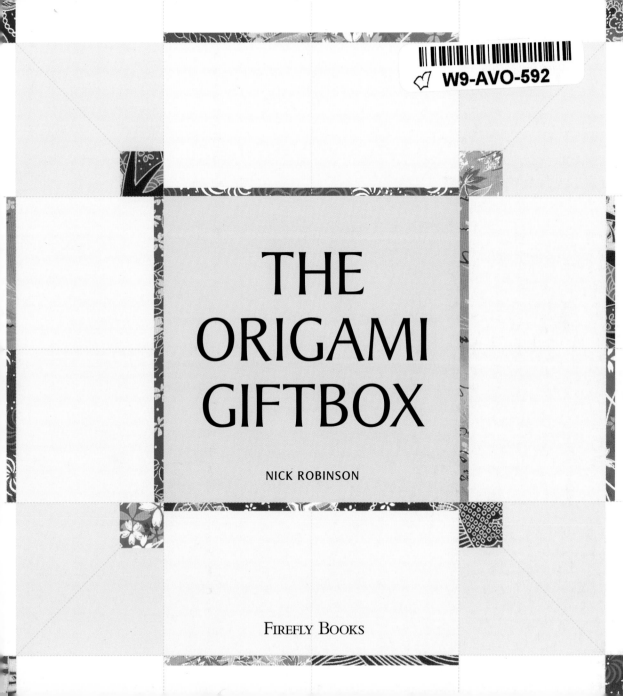

THE ORIGAMI GIFTBOX

NICK ROBINSON

FIREFLY BOOKS

A FIREFLY BOOK

Published by Firefly Books Ltd. 2006

Copyright © 2006 Quarto Inc.

First printing

Publisher Cataloging-in-Publication Data (U.S.)

Robinson, Nick, 1957-
The origami giftbox [kit] : tools, techniques and materials : everything you need to start folding today / Nick Robinson.
[64] p. : col. photos. ; cm.
Includes index.
Includes bone folder, 20 sheets of origami paper and instructional guidebook.
ISBN-13: 978-1-55407-198-2 (pbk.)
ISBN-10: 1-55407-198-4 (pbk.)
1. Origami. 2. Box making. I. Title.
736.982 dc22   TT870.R634 2006

Published in the United States by
Firefly Books (U.S.) Inc.
P.O. Box 1338, Ellicott Station
Buffalo, New York 14205

Library and Archives Canada Cataloguing in Publication

Robinson, Nick, 1957-
The origami giftbox [kit] : tools, techniques and materials : everything you need to start folding today /
Nick Robinson.
Includes index.
Includes bone folder, 20 sheets of origami paper and instructional guidebook.
ISBN-13: 978-1-55407-198-2
ISBN-10: 1-55407-198-4
1. Origami. I. Title.
TT870.R63 2006 736'.982
C2006-902572-X

Published in Canada by
Firefly Books Ltd.
66 Leek Crescent
Richmond Hill, Ontario L4B 1H1

Cover by Sideways Design

Conceived, designed, and produced by
Quarto Publishing plc
The Old Brewery
6 Blundell Street
London N7 9BH
QUAR.ORK

Project Editor Mary Groom
Art Editor Jacqueline Palmer
Designer Karin Skånberg
Photographer Philip Wilkins
Assistant Art Director Penny Cobb
Art Director Moira Clinch
Publisher Paul Carslake

Manufactured by Modern Age Repro House Ltd, Hong Kong

Printed by Midas Printing International Limited, China

CONTENTS

INTRODUCTION

▼ This intriguing geometric shape uses three sheets of differently colored paper.

Origami is a hobby that can be enjoyed by people of all ages. You don't need expensive tools, just your hands and a sheet of paper. You don't need anywhere special to fold; you could be in a lineup, on a plane or bus, sitting at home, or at the dentist's. As well as the sheer fun of making unusual things from a familiar material, many people will have encountered origami as a young child. Somewhere in the recesses of your mind, there will be happy memories waiting to surface.

Many people assume that to be a paper-folder (sometimes called an "origamist") you need higher than average levels of patience and creativity. This is not the case! There are designs at all levels, from simple to ultra-complex. While the more complicated will certainly need some dedication to complete, anyone can make and learn simple designs very easily. In fact, one of the attractions of origami is that you can make models that look very artistic, even if you don't feel especially artistic yourself! You can follow the instructions in a quite mechanical way, but still produce something that has a charm and life of its own.

In order to get the most from this book, you just need to follow some simple guidelines.

PREPARE YOUR FOLDING AREA

You should have plenty of room to lay out your book, supplies of paper, a nice cup of herbal tea (or whatever is your favorite beverage), and a flat surface upon which to fold. In addition, good lighting is essential for seeing the creases in a sheet of paper. Some folders like to have suitable relaxing music in the background.

▼ Try to choose a patterned paper that suits the final model.

▲ You will soon be able to create lifelike models, like this cicada, with ease.

▶ Chinese stars are said to bring good luck to the origamist who makes them!

PREPARE YOUR MATERIALS

It's best to practice a model using cheap paper. Then, after you have made it a few times, use a more impressive sheet. Whichever paper you use, it should be perfectly square, if at all possible. Most commercial paper is square, but you sometimes find "rogue" batches. If you are cutting paper to size, it's worth investing in a proper paper cutter. This will allow you to buy letter-sized paper cheaply in bulk and give yourself loads of practice paper.

PREPARE YOURSELF

Make sure your hands are clean and dry. Try not to fold when you are stressed or if you have an appointment in the near future—you should be relaxed and free from interruptions if possible. Fold slowly and neatly, always looking ahead at the next diagram so you can see what you are aiming at.

◀ A pair of Pixie boots can also be used to make an unusual pair of earrings!

PAPER

One of the beauties of origami is that you can fold most types of paper; as long as it can be creased and will hold that crease, you can get by. Some flimsy types, such as tissue paper, are not suitable, nor are thicker papers, but there is still a huge range to choose from. When you are working out how to make a design, all you need is a large square. Once you have mastered the folding sequence, you then need to consider the best paper with which to fold a "presentation" example.

Commercial origami paper comes in a wide variety of colors and patterns and is usually square. This is a perfect material for folding with, although it can be slightly bland and lacks any texture. It can, however, be hard to find larger sheets required for complex designs or for large display pieces. In this case, you'll need to look at buying larger sheets from art or craft stores and cutting them to a suitable size. To do this properly, you'll need a cutting board and a sharp knife.

With "art" paper, you have a wide variety, not only of colors, but also textures. Even so, it may be that you want a combination you can't find. In this case, you can laminate two different sheets together using a spray adhesive (try to avoid inhaling the fumes). Some folders like to make a laminate of tissue and foil to offer the folding qualities of foil without the crude finish. There are no rules; just try to choose a paper that is suitable for the subject. When assessing new paper, the simplest method is to fold a corner over and judge the results. The following are other types of paper worth considering.

WRAPPING PAPER

Plain brown wrapping paper is perfect for folding with and you can buy it in large rolls. More decorative wrapping paper can sometimes be found at a florist.

WASHI PAPER

Washi is handmade in Japan and is high-quality expensive paper. It is often made with typically Japanese designs and patterns.

CHIYOGAMI PAPER

Chiyogami is Japanese paper that is decorated with brightly colored, woodblock-printed patterns. There are many patterns and it is very beautiful.

MONEY

Paper money is great for origami since it is hard wearing and holds a crease well. However, you need to find designs that work from a rectangle. There are many dollar-bill designs that will work with various currencies.

CANSON

This is a specific brand of paper that comes in a wide range of useful colors. It also has a pleasing texture and is suitable for the technique known as "wet-folding," where the paper is dampened before and during folding. It then hardens as it dries out.

HOW TO FOLD

Folding paper is part of our everyday lives, but folding neatly and accurately is a skill we need to work on—it rarely comes naturally. Every crease is important, from the first to the last, but especially at the start. A small error will become a large one by the time you've finished. So you should take your time with every fold; line up the paper carefully, hold it in place with one hand, and then flatten the crease with the other hand.

Decorative paper
Using decorative paper will make your models look more impressive. Whenever you see some beautiful paper, buy it and store it carefully—over time you'll build up a useful collection so a specific model can have just the right paper.

FOLDS AND TECHNIQUES

Origami uses a common set of agreed symbols to represent common folds and techniques. These were developed around fifty years ago by Akira Yoshizawa and Samuel Randlett. In many ways, they led to the international spread of origami, since understanding the symbols means you don't really need to understand the words that may be alongside. A really good set of origami diagrams shouldn't require any words at all. However, a few well-chosen words can help you through a tricky move and they can save on diagram space.

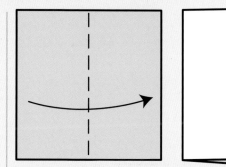

▲ **Valley fold** The arrow shows the direction in which the paper moves. This fold is usually made with the paper flat on the table, although more advanced folders sometimes fold "in the air." In general, you fold to a specific target, which may be a point, edge, or crease.

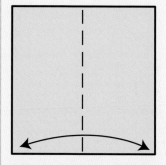

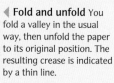

◀ **Fold and unfold** You fold a valley in the usual way, then unfold the paper to its original position. The resulting crease is indicated by a thin line.

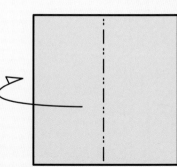

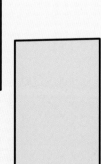

▲ **Mountain fold** The paper folds underneath itself and the fold must be done "in the air." Note the arrowhead is different from that of the valley fold. A mountain fold is often easier to make if you turn the paper upside down and make a valley fold instead, but this is not always possible.

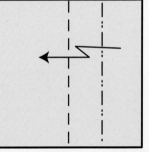

▲ **Pleat** A sequence of a valley and a mountain fold forms a pleat, where a single layer becomes three layers.

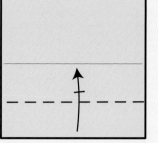

◀ **Repeat arrow** Whatever fold is shown should be repeated on a similar corner or side. Check the next diagram to see exactly where to repeat, but it should be logical. Each notch on the fold arrow indicates a single repeat.

▲ **Turn the paper over** Lift the paper up and turn it over as if you were turning the page of a book. When the arrow is rotated through 90 degrees, it indicates turning from top to bottom or vice versa.

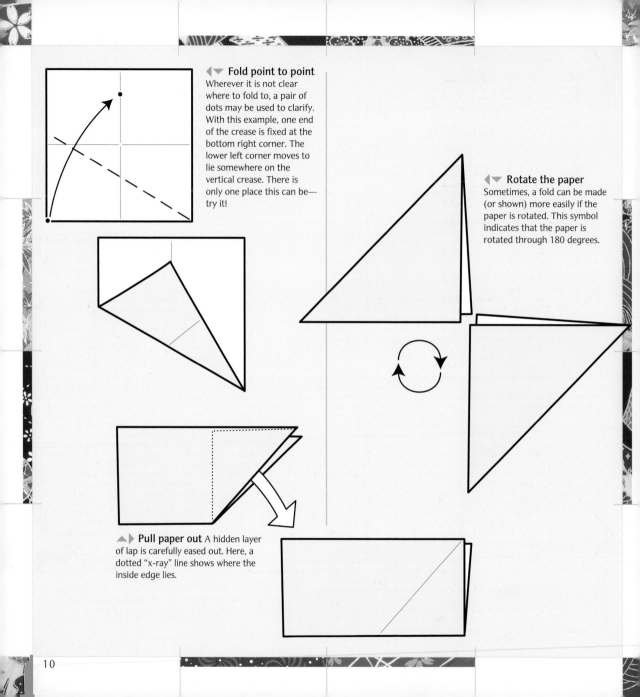

Fold point to point

Wherever it is not clear where to fold to, a pair of dots may be used to clarify. With this example, one end of the crease is fixed at the bottom right corner. The lower left corner moves to lie somewhere on the vertical crease. There is only one place this can be—try it!

Rotate the paper

Sometimes, a fold can be made (or shown) more easily if the paper is rotated. This symbol indicates that the paper is rotated through 180 degrees.

Pull paper out

A hidden layer of lap is carefully eased out. Here, a dotted "x-ray" line shows where the inside edge lies.

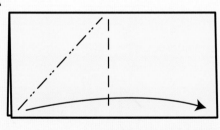

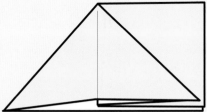

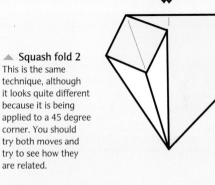

▲ **Squash fold 1** Where paper has been folded and has a "closed" corner, you can't fold either layer without "squashing" part of the paper. A thick black triangle indicates the direction you should apply pressure in. Here, a 90 degree corner is being squashed.

▲ **Squash fold 2**
This is the same technique, although it looks quite different because it is being applied to a 45 degree corner. You should try both moves and try to see how they are related.

◀ **Scale changes** As a model is folded, it generally gets smaller. If our diagrams were to also reduce in size, they would be hard to follow. This arrow makes it clear that the next and subsequent steps have been substantially increased in scale for clarity. The sequence shown where all four corners are folded to the center is known as a "blintz fold" and is used later in this book.

REVERSE FOLDS

This move seems to be difficult for origami beginners, so you should study it carefully. The "reverse" name arises because some of the folds "reverse" from mountain to valley or the other way round. It has many uses; for instance, in birds it can form beaks, legs, and feet. To make accurate reverses you should "pre-crease" the paper; in other words, put the creases in place before you actually fold them.

INSIDE REVERSE

1 Make a firm pre-crease where the reverse fold will be taking place. The dotted line shows where to fold to.

2 Open the paper out on both sides and put in the valley crease shown on both sides at the same time. The paper will "flip" inside out and flatten into the new position

3 Complete.

OUTSIDE REVERSE

1 Make a pre-crease where the reverse fold will be taking place. The dotted line shows where to fold to.

2 Carefully press the paper inside, changing the mountain crease along the spine into a valley.

3 Complete.

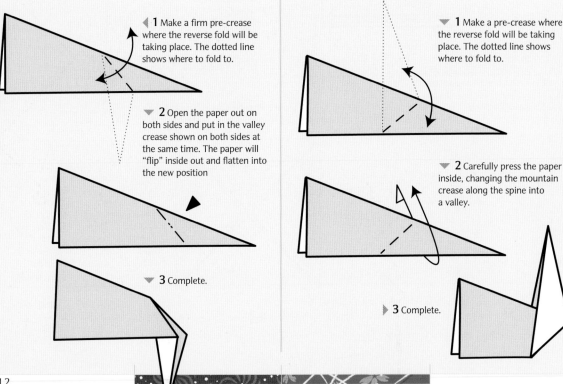

DOUBLE REVERSE FOLD

RABBIT'S EAR

This technique takes a triangular flap and forms a smaller flap at the center. Although it isn't often used to fold the ear of a rabbit, it's a good name. It can appear in various guises during a complicated origami design and is a very useful technique.

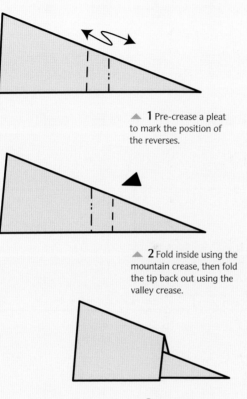

1 Pre-crease a pleat to mark the position of the reverses.

2 Fold inside using the mountain crease, then fold the tip back out using the valley crease.

3 Complete.

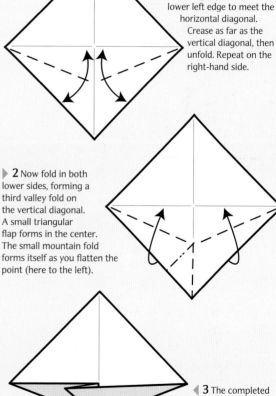

1 Start with a square, creased on both diagonals. Fold the lower left edge to meet the horizontal diagonal. Crease as far as the vertical diagonal, then unfold. Repeat on the right-hand side.

2 Now fold in both lower sides, forming a third valley fold on the vertical diagonal. A small triangular flap forms in the center. The small mountain fold forms itself as you flatten the point (here to the left).

3 The completed rabbit's ear.

BASES

PRELIMINARY BASE

This is the starting position for many origami designs, hence the name. Please study the combination of valley and mountain creases needed to form it. The easiest way to do this is to open and close the base, watching exactly what is happening.

WATERBOMB BASE

The crease pattern for the waterbomb base is exactly the same as for the preliminary base, except we collapse the paper from the other side. Try this method first, then unfold your preliminary base and "flip" it inside out.

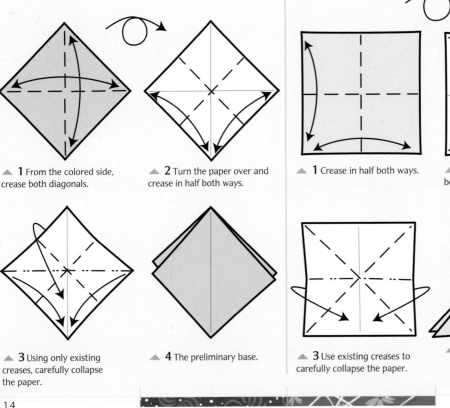
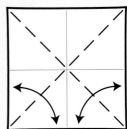
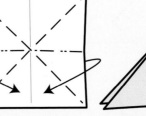

▲ **1** From the colored side, crease both diagonals.

▲ **2** Turn the paper over and crease in half both ways.

▲ **1** Crease in half both ways.

▲ **2** Turn over and crease both diagonals.

▲ **3** Using only existing creases, carefully collapse the paper.

▲ **4** The preliminary base.

▲ **3** Use existing creases to carefully collapse the paper.

▲ **4** The waterbomb base.

KITE BASE

Possibly the simplest origami base, the kite base still has a lot of creative possibilities.

BLINTZ BASE

The blintz base is folded by taking each corner of a square to the center. To find the actual center, we usually either fold side to side both ways, or add both diagonals.

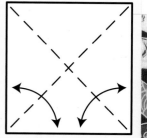

1 Fold both diagonals on a square.

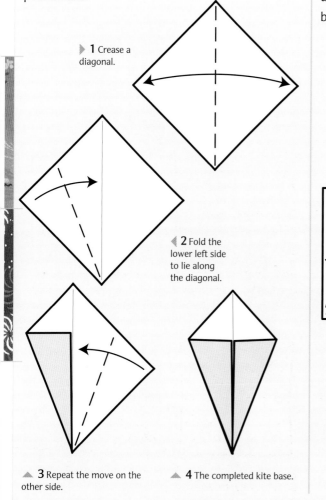

1 Crease a diagonal.

2 Fold the lower left side to lie along the diagonal.

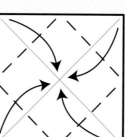

2 Fold each corner in turn to the center. Try to be very accurate!

3 Repeat the move on the other side.

4 The completed kite base.

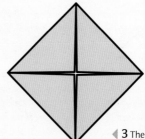

3 The completed blintz base.

THE PROJECTS

CUP

This cup is a traditional design. In Japan, children use it to hold candies, but you can also use it as a cup. Don't leave it too long before drinking! This is a perfect design for beginners, since every fold can be exactly located—there are no steps that require judgment from the folder. In step 7, an alternative is to tuck the triangular flaps inside the pocket of the flap on either side. The cup is then fully colored on the outside.

Take your time, making sure the paper is in exactly the right place before making the crease. When you are familiar with the method, you can cut out step 2 altogether, and at step 3 make a light pinch to mark where the crease meets the edge—it's all you need. With several of the designs in this book, there are ways to fold them with fewer creases, once you know what you are doing. Origami generally looks better with as few creases as possible on the finished design.

1 Start with a square, white side toward you. Fold the lower corner to the top corner.

2 Fold the upper right edge to the lower edge, crease, and unfold.

3 Turn the paper over. Fold the upper left edge to the lower edge, crease, and unfold.

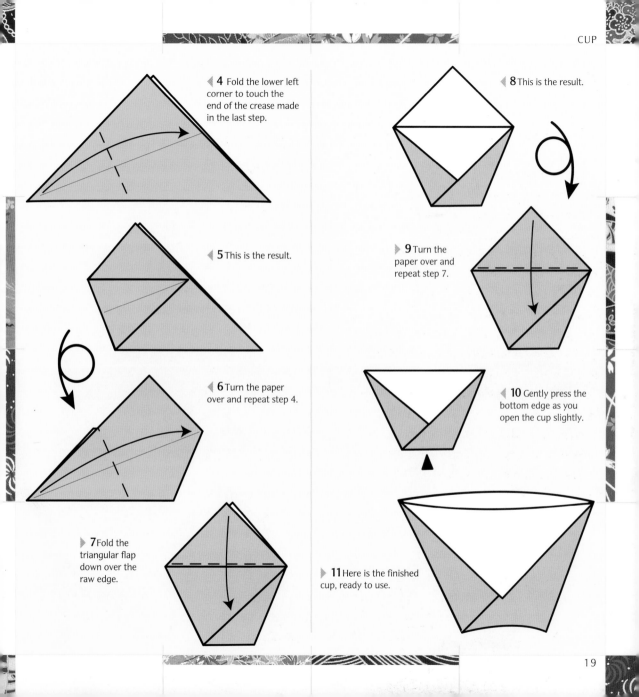

4 Fold the lower left corner to touch the end of the crease made in the last step.

5 This is the result.

6 Turn the paper over and repeat step 4.

7 Fold the triangular flap down over the raw edge.

8 This is the result.

9 Turn the paper over and repeat step 7.

10 Gently press the bottom edge as you open the cup slightly.

11 Here is the finished cup, ready to use.

19

CICADA

This is a traditional Japanese design. These extraordinary insects live underground for 17 years, then emerge in their millions to produce an amazing sound that you can hear on every street in Japanese cities. By altering the angle of the creases in steps 6 and 7, you can produce many different proportions. You can also make the finished insect slightly 3D by emphasizing the mountain crease down the center of the back.

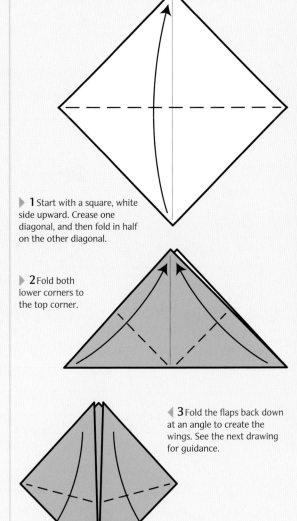

▶ **1** Start with a square, white side upward. Crease one diagonal, and then fold in half on the other diagonal.

▶ **2** Fold both lower corners to the top corner.

◀ **3** Fold the flaps back down at an angle to create the wings. See the next drawing for guidance.

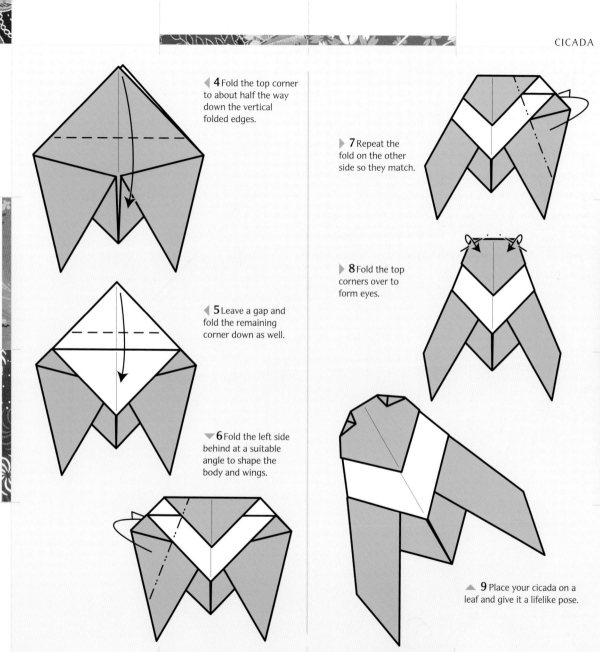

◀ **4** Fold the top corner to about half the way down the vertical folded edges.

▶ **7** Repeat the fold on the other side so they match.

▶ **8** Fold the top corners over to form eyes.

◀ **5** Leave a gap and fold the remaining corner down as well.

▼ **6** Fold the left side behind at a suitable angle to shape the body and wings.

▲ **9** Place your cicada on a leaf and give it a lifelike pose.

FRENCH FRY BOAT

This is a variation of a traditional design I saw during a rare visit to a takeout restaurant. The assistant had been shown it by her employer, who had learned it from a friend many years ago. It's always interesting to keep your eyes open for examples of origami that are used in a practical way, such as newspaper hats or envelopes. Many of these are widely known, even by people who don't consider that they know any "proper" origami.

To an experienced paper-folder, the finished model looks like a traditional boat, but it uses a completely different technique. This particular design had a slightly untidy finish (in origami terms!), so I reworked it slightly.

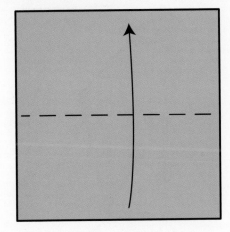

▲ **1** Start with a square of paper, colored side upward. Fold in half from bottom to top.

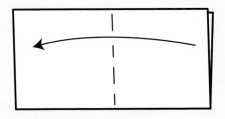

▲ **2** Fold in half from right to left.

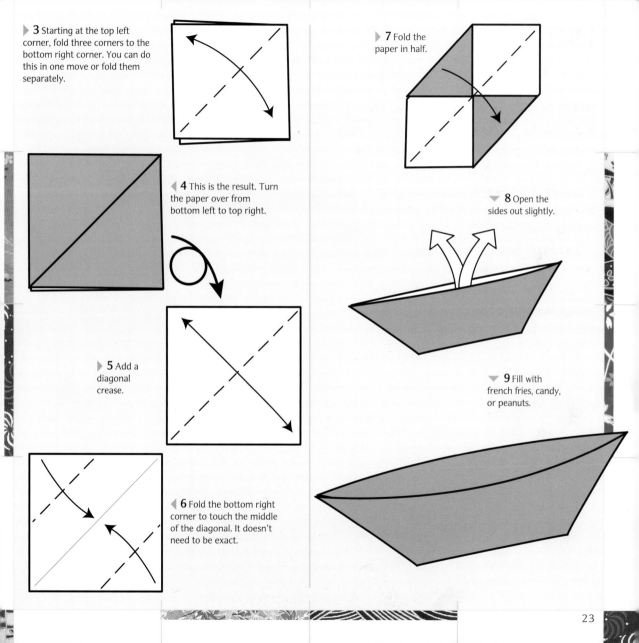

▶ **3** Starting at the top left corner, fold three corners to the bottom right corner. You can do this in one move or fold them separately.

◀ **4** This is the result. Turn the paper over from bottom left to top right.

▶ **5** Add a diagonal crease.

◀ **6** Fold the bottom right corner to touch the middle of the diagonal. It doesn't need to be exact.

▶ **7** Fold the paper in half.

▼ **8** Open the sides out slightly.

▼ **9** Fill with french fries, candy, or peanuts.

GLIDER

This is a variation on a traditional design by a Japanese paper plane expert called Eiji Nakamura. He had the inspired idea of locking the lower flaps together so they didn't unfold during flight. This design is very stable in flight. You can try folding the wings further down at step 6 and see how this affects the flight characteristics.

When launching a plane, there are three basic things you can alter: first, the angle of the wings (known technically as "dihedral"); second, you can launch at different speeds; third, you can launch at different angles. Each of these factors will affect the flight and every plane will have a "best" combination that you can find only by experimenting.

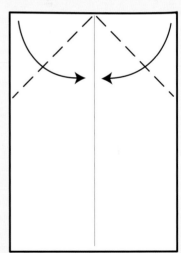

1 Start with a letter-sized paper, creased in half on the short edge. Fold both halves of the short edge in to lie on the vertical crease.

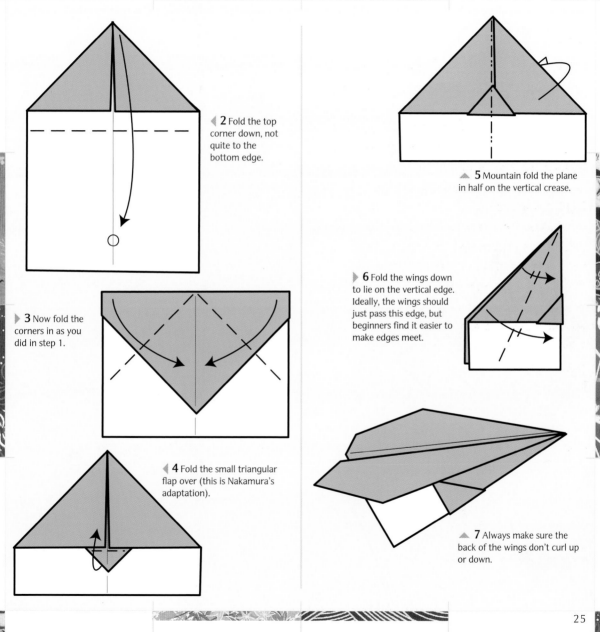

◀ **2** Fold the top corner down, not quite to the bottom edge.

▶ **3** Now fold the corners in as you did in step 1.

◀ **4** Fold the small triangular flap over (this is Nakamura's adaptation).

▲ **5** Mountain fold the plane in half on the vertical crease.

▶ **6** Fold the wings down to lie on the vertical edge. Ideally, the wings should just pass this edge, but beginners find it easier to make edges meet.

▲ **7** Always make sure the back of the wings don't curl up or down.

CAT BROOCH

Some creators decide on the subject before they start to fold. Others, like myself, prefer to play with the paper and see what subjects can be found by making obvious or pleasing creases. I "saw" the cat's head fairly quickly, but wanted to make good use of the flap behind, as a pin for a brooch. As I folded it in half, I realized there was a pocket I could tuck it into, which was neat.

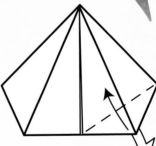

1 Start with a square of paper, colored side upward, with a diagonal crease in place. Fold both lower sides to the crease.

2 Turn the paper over and fold the sharp corner to the opposite corner.

3 Make a crease from the right-hand corner to the center of the lower edge, allowing the corner underneath to "flip" out.

4 Like this. Repeat the step on the left side.

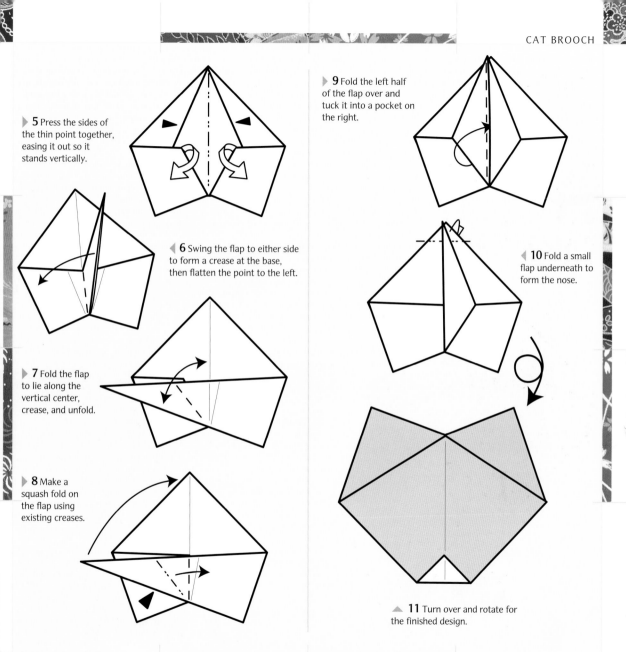

5 Press the sides of the thin point together, easing it out so it stands vertically.

6 Swing the flap to either side to form a crease at the base, then flatten the point to the left.

7 Fold the flap to lie along the vertical center, crease, and unfold.

8 Make a squash fold on the flap using existing creases.

9 Fold the left half of the flap over and tuck it into a pocket on the right.

10 Fold a small flap underneath to form the nose.

11 Turn over and rotate for the finished design.

STAR

This design is an example of how origami designs can inspire new creators to adapt and extend the work of others. The American Mette Pederson has produced many books devoted to origami rings (wreaths, rather than the kind you wear on your finger!). One of these rings inspired the German Carmen Sprung to produce a design called "Gudrun's Star" using a 3:2 rectangle. I saw this design and worked out a method of creating the same result from a letter-size rectangle.

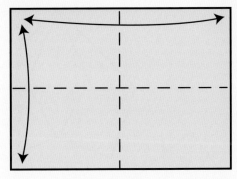

▲ **1** Start with a letter-size sheet, colored side (if any) upward. Crease in half both ways.

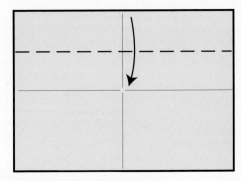

▲ **2** Fold the upper edge to the center.

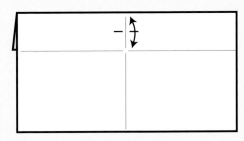

▲ **3** Turn the paper over and make a small crease to mark the halfway point of the upper section.

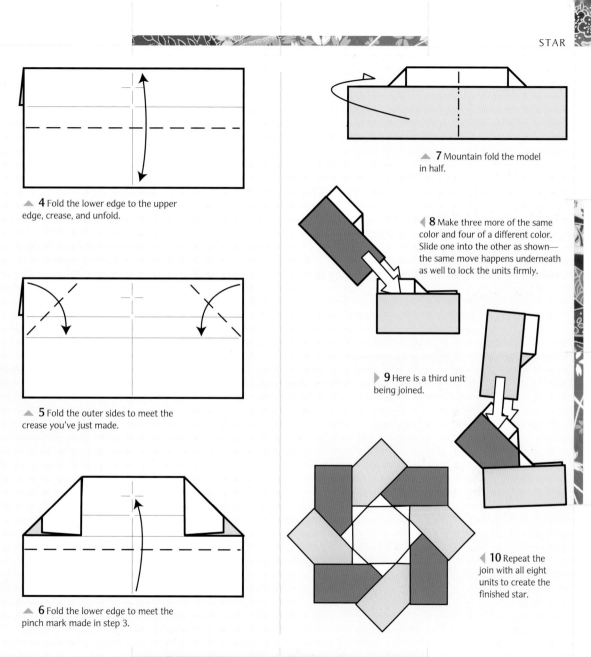

▲ **4** Fold the lower edge to the upper edge, crease, and unfold.

▲ **5** Fold the outer sides to meet the crease you've just made.

▲ **6** Fold the lower edge to meet the pinch mark made in step 3.

▲ **7** Mountain fold the model in half.

◀ **8** Make three more of the same color and four of a different color. Slide one into the other as shown— the same move happens underneath as well to lock the units firmly.

▶ **9** Here is a third unit being joined.

◀ **10** Repeat the join with all eight units to create the finished star.

FISH

Several years ago, I was trying to teach an aircraft design to my friend. Halfway through, I forgot the steps. My friend played around with the layers and suddenly said, "It's a fish!" And it was. Sometimes a fresh eye and fertile imagination can see new possibilities in a set of creases.

It is an example of how simple origami seeks to capture the basic form of a subject and not focus too much on the fine detail. Like any art form, origami has a full range, from very simple to highly complex. Paper folders usually prefer a certain level of difficulty, but few would argue over whether one style is better than another—it's simply a matter of personal taste.

1 Start with a square, white side upward. Crease and unfold both diagonals.

2 Fold two opposite corners to the center.

3 This is the result. Turn the paper over.

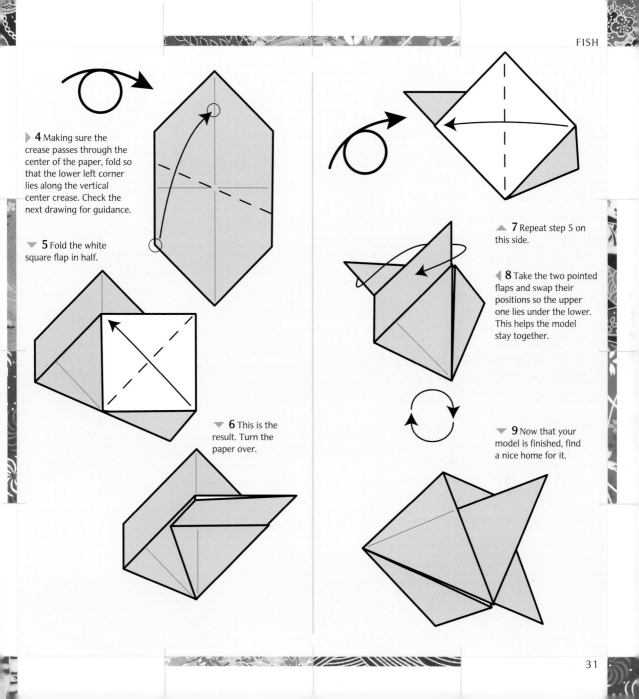

4 Making sure the crease passes through the center of the paper, fold so that the lower left corner lies along the vertical center crease. Check the next drawing for guidance.

5 Fold the white square flap in half.

6 This is the result. Turn the paper over.

7 Repeat step 5 on this side.

8 Take the two pointed flaps and swap their positions so the upper one lies under the lower. This helps the model stay together.

9 Now that your model is finished, find a nice home for it.

CATERPILLAR

Where a subject has several identical sections, it can often be simpler to create separate "units" that slot into each other. The alternative would be to use a long strip of paper, a solution that is not very common in origami terms. Some origami philosophers may argue that a long single sheet of paper is "purer" than using several squares, but to my mind the simplest solution is generally the best.

2 This shape is known as the "kite base." Fold the lower point to where the two colored corners meet, crease firmly, and unfold.

▶ **3** A cunning move here. On the left side, lift open the first layer slightly. On the right side, make a valley fold using an existing crease. As it folds in, make an inside reverse fold (see Reverse Folds, page 12) on the left-hand side.

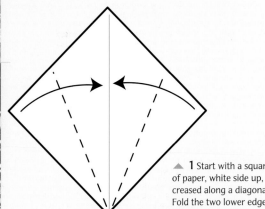

1 Start with a square of paper, white side up, creased along a diagonal. Fold the two lower edges to the diagonal crease.

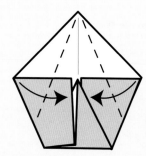

◀ **4** Fold the upper white edges to the center crease.

5 Fold the paper in half from left to right, tucking the flap on the left into the pocket on the right.

6 This is the complete body section. Make lots and lots more!

9 Fold the corners over so the edges lie along the creases.

7 Turn the paper around to this position. This shows how the body joins together—just tuck the point into the pocket.

10 Mountain fold along the center.

11 Inside reverse the tip of the white flap.

12 Valley fold the point and tuck it inside the head.

8 To make the head, fold the body up to step 4, unfold the last step, then turn the paper over.

13 Open the head into 3D along the crease shown. Tuck the head into the body.

14 Enjoy the caterpillar—but don't expect it to turn into a butterfly!

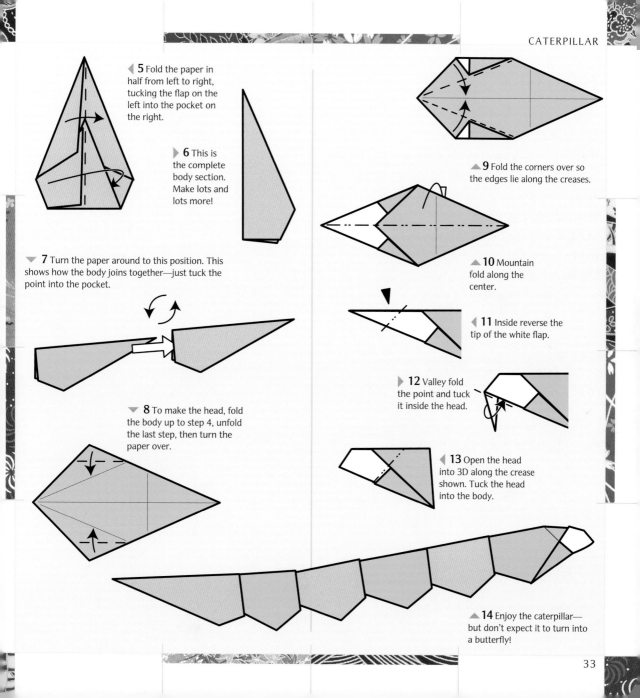

SCOTTY DOG

This is a design by the American folder and magician Robert Neale. His work is characterized by an elegance and humor that are often best appreciated by more experienced folders. This design is an almost perfect piece of origami. A few simple folds and an easily recognizable Scotty dog emerges, but you don't know what it is until the very last fold!

1 Start with a square, white side upward. Crease a diagonal, and then make a light pinch to mark the halfway point of the diagonal.

2 Fold each end of the diagonal into the center.

3 Leaving a gap, fold one corner back out to form the tail. Tuck the other corner underneath a little.

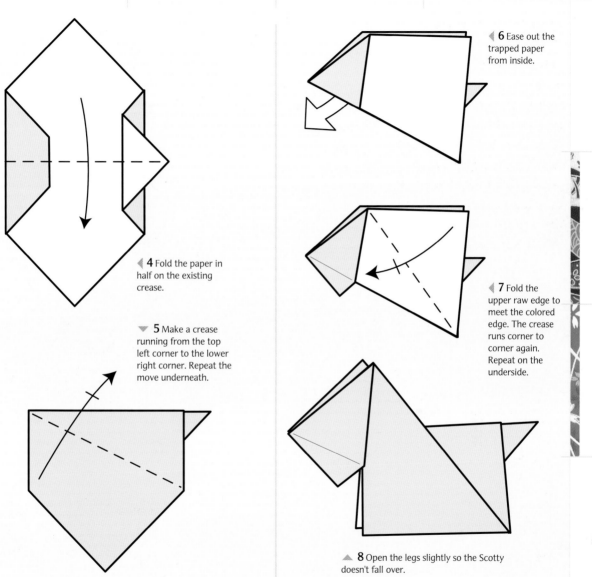

4 Fold the paper in half on the existing crease.

5 Make a crease running from the top left corner to the lower right corner. Repeat the move underneath.

6 Ease out the trapped paper from inside.

7 Fold the upper raw edge to meet the colored edge. The crease runs corner to corner again. Repeat on the underside.

8 Open the legs slightly so the Scotty doesn't fall over.

FIRST FLIGHT

Many origami designs are static—accurate, clever, but lacking in life or spirit. It's important that when folding a "living" subject, we try to capture some of that spirit in the folding of the model. This is a design that went through several revisions, adding extra complexity and features, before having them stripped away to reveal the simple, stylized version you see here. When designing origami, it's always good to question whether adding extra details improves or detracts from the finished design.

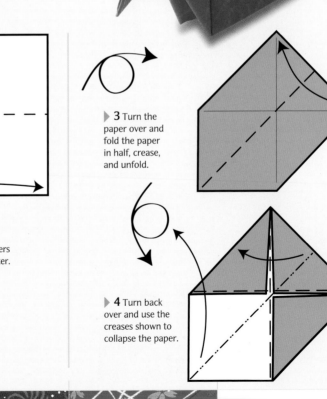

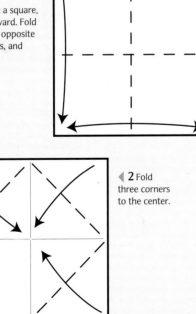

▶ **1** Start with a square, white side upward. Fold in half, side to opposite side, both ways, and unfold.

◀ **2** Fold three corners to the center.

▶ **3** Turn the paper over and fold the paper in half, crease, and unfold.

▶ **4** Turn back over and use the creases shown to collapse the paper.

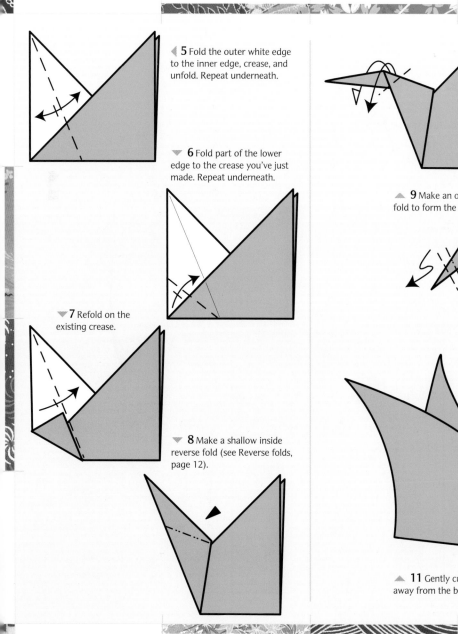

5 Fold the outer white edge to the inner edge, crease, and unfold. Repeat underneath.

6 Fold part of the lower edge to the crease you've just made. Repeat underneath.

7 Refold on the existing crease.

8 Make a shallow inside reverse fold (see Reverse folds, page 12).

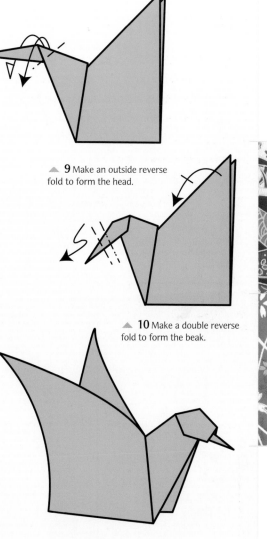

9 Make an outside reverse fold to form the head.

10 Make a double reverse fold to form the beak.

11 Gently curl the wings away from the body.

PIXIE BOOTS

This is a design which works as well using a table napkin folded
in half, a dollar bill, or half a square of paper. In order to make
both left- and right-handed boots, you need to repeat certain
moves with a mirror image. These boots look superb if you make
them from tiny sheets of paper, fasten them together, and hang
them on a Christmas tree.

▼ **1** Start with a 2:1 rectangle
(half a square) and fold the
short edges together. Crease
and unfold.

▼ **2** Fold the long edges
together.

◀ **3** Fold each half of the
left edge over at 45 degrees,
so that it lines up with the
central crease.

▼ **4** Fold the shorter folded
edges (on the left) to lie on the
horizontal center.

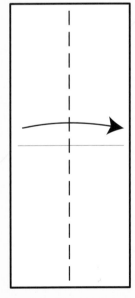

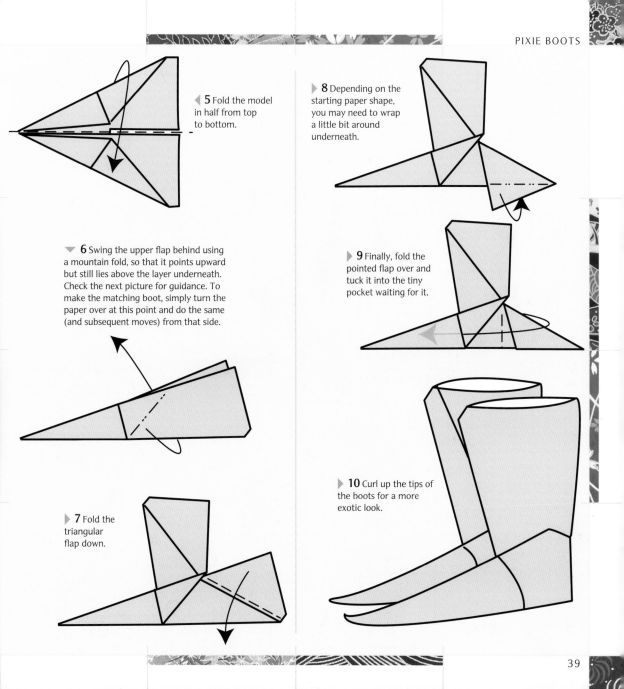

5 Fold the model in half from top to bottom.

6 Swing the upper flap behind using a mountain fold, so that it points upward but still lies above the layer underneath. Check the next picture for guidance. To make the matching boot, simply turn the paper over at this point and do the same (and subsequent moves) from that side.

7 Fold the triangular flap down.

8 Depending on the starting paper shape, you may need to wrap a little bit around underneath.

9 Finally, fold the pointed flap over and tuck it into the tiny pocket waiting for it.

10 Curl up the tips of the boots for a more exotic look.

ENVELOPE

The idea with any origami envelope is to seal the contents such that it can be sent through the mail and, additionally, to use an elegant folding sequence. This design has passed the first test and I feel meets the second as well, although I'm biased. Use the stamp to add extra security to the final move.

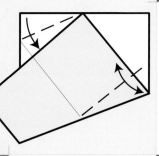

Mr Jones
12 Seaview Road
South Beach

◀ **1** Start with a letter-size rectangle. Fold the two long edges together, crease, and unfold.

▼ **2** Fold the lower right corner to the center of the top edge.

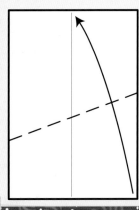

▶ **3** Fold the corner on the left to touch the center of the top edge, crease, and unfold.

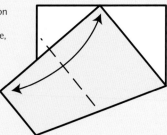

▶ **4** Fold the left half of the upper edge to lie on the nearest raw edge. Fold the right corner back along the raw edge, starting the crease where the original halfway crease meets the edge. Crease and unfold.

5 Fold the lower layer in the top right over the raw edge, crease, and unfold.

6 Unfold the large upper layer.

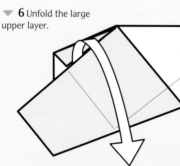

7 Refold the paper, first A, then B, using only existing creases. Some of these creases need to be altered from valley to mountain and vice versa.

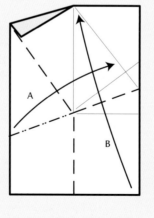

8 Inside reverse fold the lower right corner on existing creases.

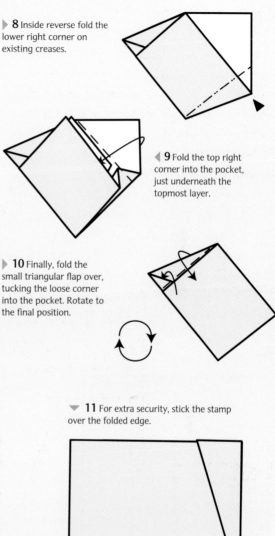

9 Fold the top right corner into the pocket, just underneath the topmost layer.

10 Finally, fold the small triangular flap over, tucking the loose corner into the pocket. Rotate to the final position.

11 For extra security, stick the stamp over the folded edge.

HEART

This heart was designed in response to a challenge from Francis Ow of Singapore. He decided to gather together many designs based on a "heart" theme and used them in a series of self-published collections. As well as creating over one hundred of his own designs, creative folders from around the world took up the challenge.

   You should fold carefully and neatly—there are several steps in this design you may need to spend some time perfecting (such as steps 4 and 11). When you have completed steps like these, unfold and refold them until you understand exactly how they work and how the diagram is explaining them. The next time you see a similar move it will then be far easier.

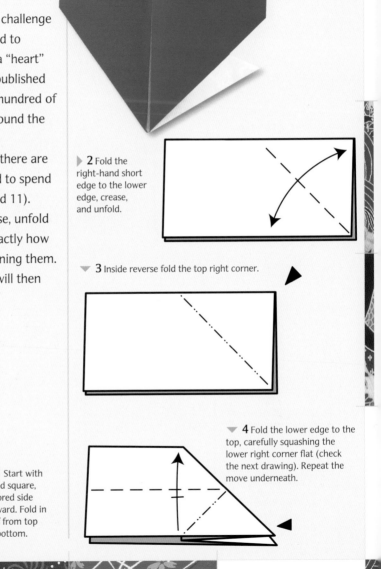

▶ **2** Fold the right-hand short edge to the lower edge, crease, and unfold.

▼ **3** Inside reverse fold the top right corner.

▼ **4** Fold the lower edge to the top, carefully squashing the lower right corner flat (check the next drawing). Repeat the move underneath.

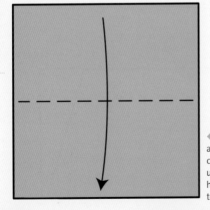

◀ **1** Start with a red square, colored side upward. Fold in half from top to bottom.

5 Fold the upper edges to the vertical edge, crease, and unfold.

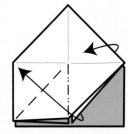

6 Inside reverse fold all the flaps at the same time.

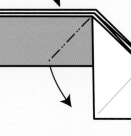

7 Fold the upper right section to the left, and fold the lower left section behind to the right.

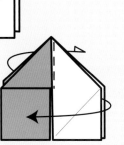

8 Fold the lower edge to the top point, crease, and unfold.

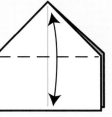

9 Crease, and then inside reverse fold the lower right corner.

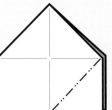

10 Make a valley fold diagonally in the white square. The paper forms into 3D.

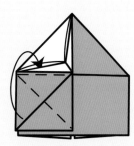

11 Lift the square colored flap up and tuck a triangular flap into the pocket. This completes the base.

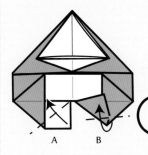

12 Fold the lower edge to the halfway point, carefully squashing the corners into triangular flaps.

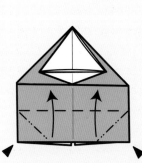

13 Make folds A, then B to round the tips.

A   B

14 Turn over for the completed heart.

PTEROSAUR

There are plenty of origami dinosaurs on hand, but few of them actually "do" anything. I enjoy action models and so set about creating one. However, what actually happened was that I created a static dino, and then noticed that if you pulled the wings apart (gently!) it nodded its beak up and down. Happy accidents are central to how many people create origami. You seem to find a design that was just waiting to be discovered.

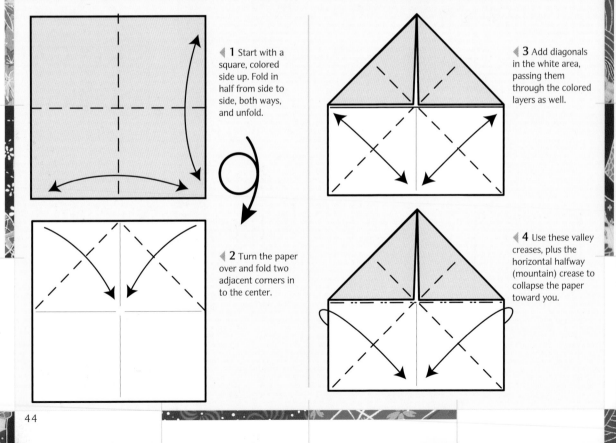

◀ **1** Start with a square, colored side up. Fold in half from side to side, both ways, and unfold.

◀ **2** Turn the paper over and fold two adjacent corners in to the center.

◀ **3** Add diagonals in the white area, passing them through the colored layers as well.

◀ **4** Use these valley creases, plus the horizontal halfway (mountain) crease to collapse the paper toward you.

5 Fold the lower edges of the square section in to the vertical center.

6 Fold the small triangle at the top behind, and then open the flaps again.

7 Lift up the first layer at the bottom corner and fold it all the way upward. The sides move inward and flatten neatly, with any luck.

8 Fold the model in half from left to right.

9 Hold the paper where shown and gently ease forward the lower section, allowing the paper to wrap around slightly. Check the next drawing.

10 Fold both wings over.

11 Fold each of the three sides of the wing to meet the adjacent side, creasing as far as the center.

12 As you peck the beak, don't forget to make the sound of a dinosaur!

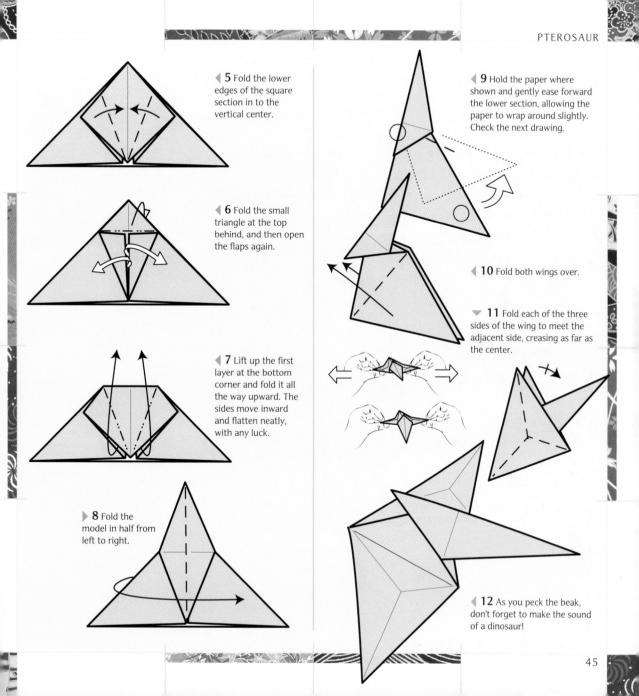

LUCKY STAR

This design is a development of a principle that has been around for over a hundred years—that you can produce a perfect pentagon by tying a knot in a strip of paper. This version adds extra layers to the pentagon, so that it can be gently squeezed into 3D. If you hold the paper up to a light at step 3, you can see a pentagonal star through it!

◀ **1** Start with a strip of paper about 8–11 inches (20–27 cm) long and between ⅜–½ inch (3–10 mm) wide. Gently tie a simple knot as shown.

▶ **2** Continue to pull the strips through, adjusting the paper so just a short strip sticks out at the bottom.

◀ **3** Eventually, you produce this knot.

▶ **4** Turn the paper over and fold the short section of paper under the first layer.

▶ **5** Turn the paper over and pull the loose strip all the way through in the same way.

▶ **6** Turn the paper over and fold the loose strip over the top of all layers.

▼ **7** Turn the paper over and fold the loose strip through as before.

◀ **8** Repeat these steps until you have a short section left, which you tuck under a layer.

▶ **9** Carefully and gently squeeze the sides to make the star three-dimensional.

▲ **10** You might have to make a few before you produce perfect examples, but it's worth the effort.

GONDOLA

This is a traditional design that has not been widely published, but it is a wonderful example of what is known as a "climactic" design. This means (like the Scotty dog earlier in this book) that you don't know what the finished model looks like until the very last step. It also incorporates an interesting and unusual folding sequence. You should be careful at step 8.

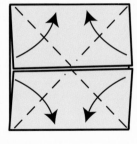

1 Start with a blintz base (see Bases, page 15) with the color on the outside. Fold two opposite sides to the center. The next step is enlarged.

3 Fold the outer edges, to the upper and lower edges respectively.

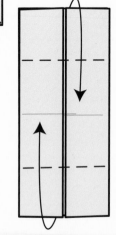

2 Fold the two short edges to the center. The next step is also enlarged.

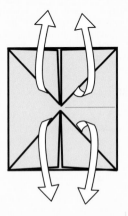

4 Pull the outer triangular flaps out and upward, leaving the central flap where it is.

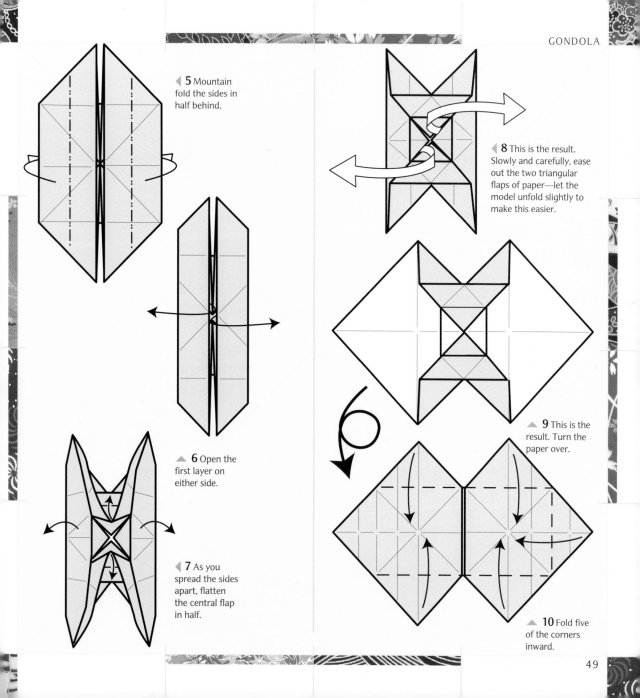

5 Mountain fold the sides in half behind.

8 This is the result. Slowly and carefully, ease out the two triangular flaps of paper—let the model unfold slightly to make this easier.

6 Open the first layer on either side.

7 As you spread the sides apart, flatten the central flap in half.

9 This is the result. Turn the paper over.

10 Fold five of the corners inward.

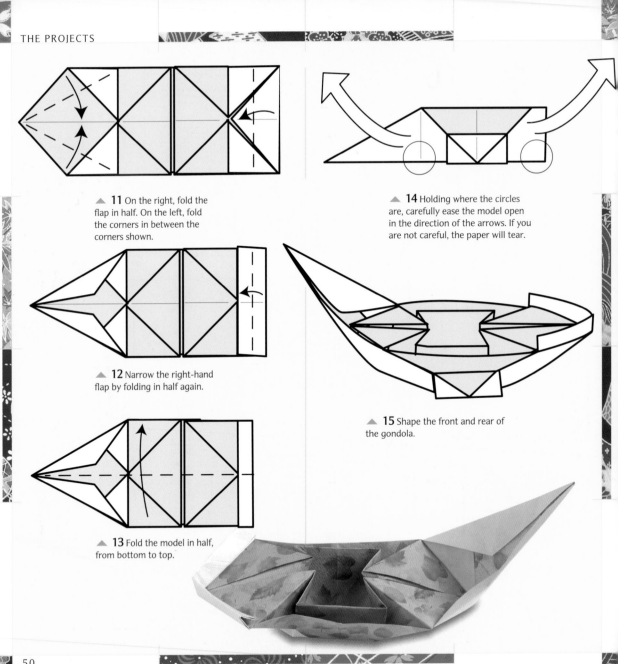

▲ **11** On the right, fold the flap in half. On the left, fold the corners in between the corners shown.

▲ **12** Narrow the right-hand flap by folding in half again.

▲ **13** Fold the model in half, from bottom to top.

▲ **14** Holding where the circles are, carefully ease the model open in the direction of the arrows. If you are not careful, the paper will tear.

▲ **15** Shape the front and rear of the gondola.

3D CUBE ILLUSION

This is an origami version of a well-known optical illusion. Does the cube appear to point toward you, or is it "hollow"? It turned out that the underside was attractive as well. To find the 60 degree angles needed, it's necessary to add creases that spoil the clean face of the final design. In order to make it without them, you should fold a template, which will produce the proper angle.

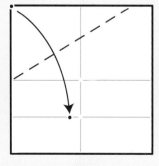

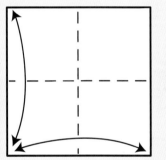

◀ **1** Start with a square, white side up. Fold from side to side, both ways.

▼ **2** Fold the lower side in to the center, crease, and unfold.

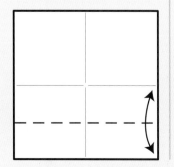

▶ **3** Starting the crease in the center of the left edge, fold over so the upper left corner meets the lower quarter crease on the left. Check the next illustration for guidance.

▶ **4** This is the template you need to fold the units.

▼ **5** Wrap another identical square around the template to copy the crease onto it. Unfold, then rotate the paper 180 degrees, and repeat. This should be the crease pattern you produce. Fold on the left-hand crease.

▶ **6** Fold half of the upper edge to meet the remaining crease.

◀ **7** Fold the other half to meet the colored edge, crease, and unfold.

▶ **8** Fold part of the right edge to meet the most recent crease.

◀ **9** Now fold over the flap on the right.

▶ **10** Fold over the remaining white section.

◀ **11** Fold the lower triangle in half from left to right, crease, and unfold.

▶ **12** Fold the short raw edge to meet the vertical crease.

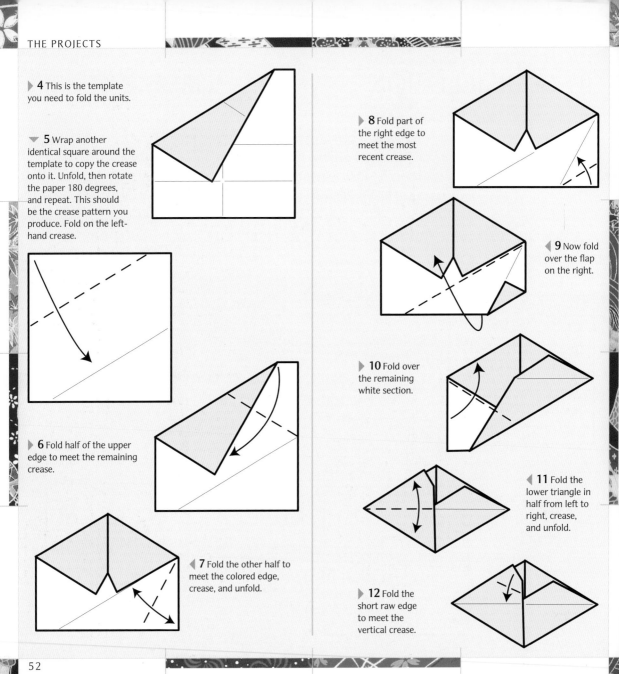

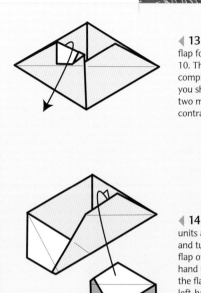

13 Unfold the flap folded in step 10. This is the completed unit—you should fold two more with contrasting colors.

14 Arrange two units as shown and tuck a hidden flap of the right-hand unit behind the flap on the left-hand unit.

15 Fold all layers behind on the mountain crease shown.

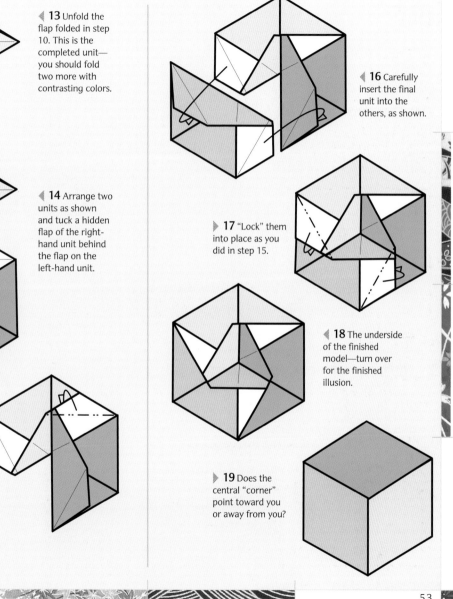

16 Carefully insert the final unit into the others, as shown.

17 "Lock" them into place as you did in step 15.

18 The underside of the finished model—turn over for the finished illusion.

19 Does the central "corner" point toward you or away from you?

IRIS

This is a variation of a traditional model. Here, instead of starting with a square, we start with an equilateral triangle, giving us three petals instead of the usual four. The geometry of a triangle gives us angles of 15, 30, and 60 degrees, very different from the 22.5, 45, and 90 degrees offered by a square. An English folder called Lord Brill has created a magnificent horse from an equilateral triangle (you can see some examples of his work on the British Origami Society website, www.britishorigami.info).

We make two identical flowers, then insert one in the other to create a six-pointed flower. To curl the leaves you should use the edge of a ruler and drag the flap over it at a sharp angle, known as "scoring." When you can make this model properly, see if you can work out how to fold it from a square of paper—the techniques are identical, but the angles change. If you know how to make a pentagonal sheet of paper, try folding it from that! Folding a familiar design from a different starting shape can open up many new possibilities.

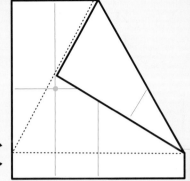

▲ **1** Start with a square, white on both sides. In order to create a triangular sheet of paper, start with step 4 of the 3D illusion design and fold the other two sides over before cutting along the dotted lines.

▲ **2** Rotate the paper to the angle shown, crease in half in each direction, then fold in half from top to bottom.

▲ **3** Inside reverse fold the top corner.

▲ **4** Fold the first flap to point downward along the vertical crease.

5 Fold the narrow flap in half, crease, and unfold back to step 4.

6 Fold the lower left edge to the vertical crease, making a crease only where shown. Unfold again.

7 Open and squash the flap (see Folds and Techniques, page 11).

8 Lift the flap, forming a petal fold.

9 Repeat steps 4–8 on the other two flaps.

10 Fold each of the three flaps downward.

11 Fold the two upper edges to the center crease. Repeat on the other two flaps.

12 Open and curl the three petals outward, opening the flower into 3D. Insert one flower into the other.

13 You can curl the petals by scoring them with the edge of a ruler.

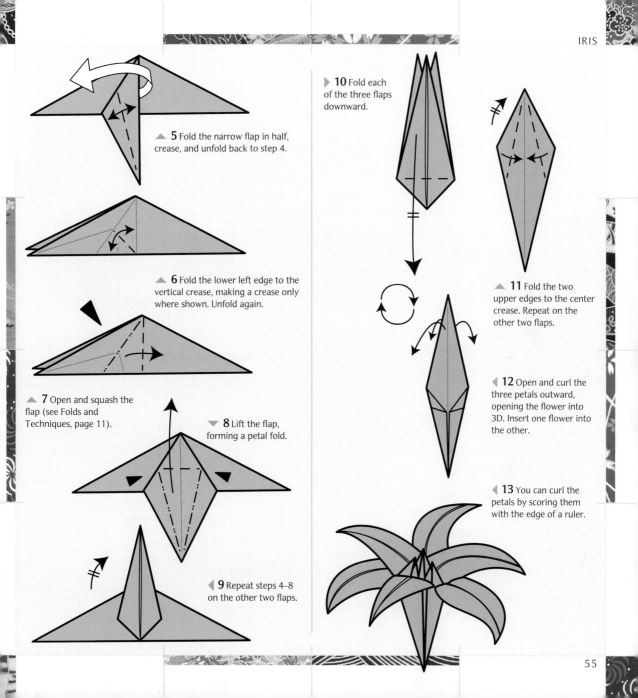

FISH RING

This is an excellent example of how one origami design can lead to another. I was playing with two fish designs when I realized one could slip into the other and that I could use the tail flaps to "lock" two together. Given enough fishes, it was possible to form an octagonal ring. There are many such rings in the origami world and generally, when you have a "flat" ring, you can remove one or more elements to form a 3D version! Why not try it out with this design? As with all such rings, you need to fold very accurately to produce a strong finish.

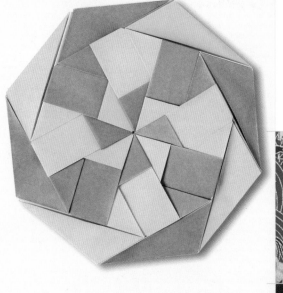

▶ **1** Fold eight fishes (see page 30) as far as step 7 (it's important not to fold step 8), then arrange two (with contrasting colors) as shown. One will slide into the other a little way.

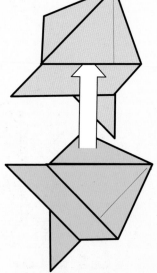

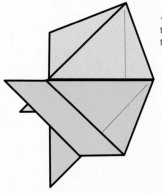

◀ **2** Like this. Hold the two firmly together and turn the paper over.

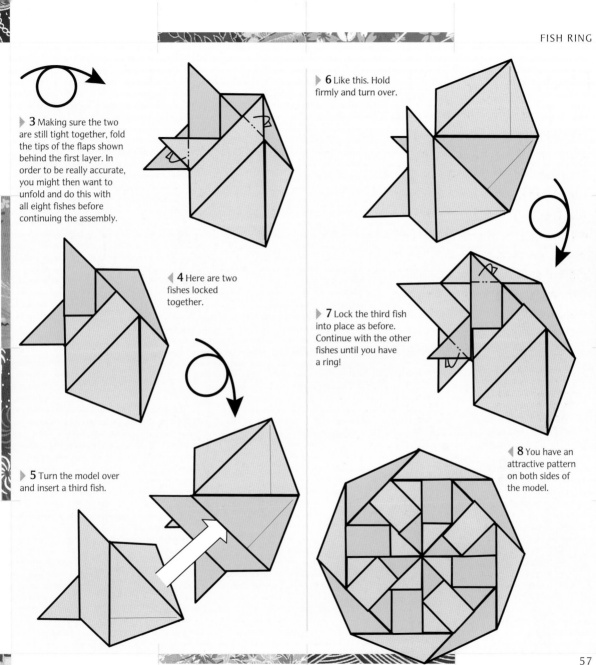

3 Making sure the two are still tight together, fold the tips of the flaps shown behind the first layer. In order to be really accurate, you might then want to unfold and do this with all eight fishes before continuing the assembly.

4 Here are two fishes locked together.

5 Turn the model over and insert a third fish.

6 Like this. Hold firmly and turn over.

7 Lock the third fish into place as before. Continue with the other fishes until you have a ring!

8 You have an attractive pattern on both sides of the model.

STILETTO HEELS

This elegant design is by the South American folder, Roman Díaz. Shoes are quite a popular subject in origami, and some can even be worn if they are made from newspapers. I wouldn't risk it with this design, though. It starts with the kite base, a popular starting point for many simple designs. Can you see how a swan could be folded starting at step 7?

The design also shows that origami need not worry about the function of an object, just the form. Here, there is no "hole" in which to put your feet. This is far less important than the fact that the design captures the smooth lines of this type of shoe. In order to create a more "practical" design, we would have to compromise the clean lines and folding sequence of the model.

▷ **1** Start with a square, white side upward, creased along a diagonal. Fold both sides to the vertical crease.

◁ **2** Fold in half from bottom to top, crease, and unfold.

▷ **3** Fold the lower left edge to lie on the crease made in the last step. Repeat on the right.

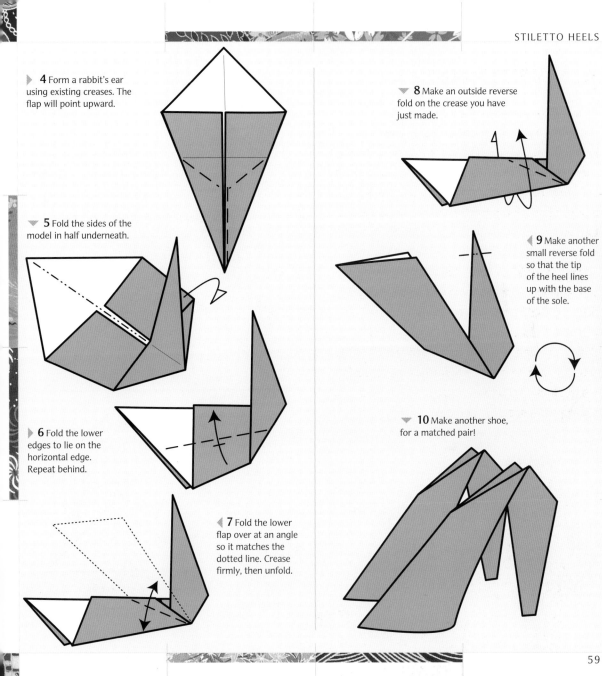

▶ **4** Form a rabbit's ear using existing creases. The flap will point upward.

▼ **5** Fold the sides of the model in half underneath.

▶ **6** Fold the lower edges to lie on the horizontal edge. Repeat behind.

◀ **7** Fold the lower flap over at an angle so it matches the dotted line. Crease firmly, then unfold.

▼ **8** Make an outside reverse fold on the crease you have just made.

◀ **9** Make another small reverse fold so that the tip of the heel lines up with the base of the sole.

▼ **10** Make another shoe, for a matched pair!

WATER TANK

This is a typical design from the late Philip Shen. Beginning in the 1960s, he created elegant geometric designs that utilize a method known as "pre-creasing." This means that you make most, if not all, of the creases necessary to complete the model in advance. By step 6 of this design, you have prepared all the creases you need and can begin the actual folding. The advantage of this approach is that you are able to make sharp, accurate creases while the paper is flat. Assembly is therefore much easier and neater.

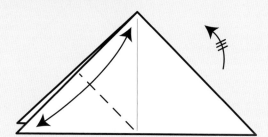

▲ **1** Start with a waterbomb base (see Bases, page 14). Fold the lower left corner to the top corner, crease, and unfold. Repeat on the other three corners.

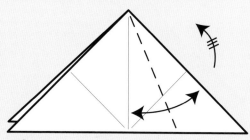

▲ **2** Fold the upper right edge to the center, crease, and unfold. Repeat on the other three corners.

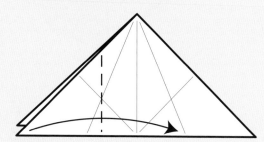

▲ **3** Fold the lower left corner to meet the crease made in the last step.

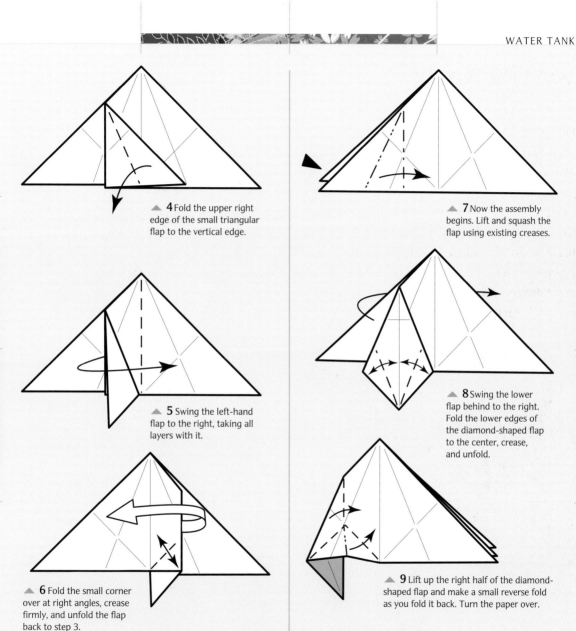

4 Fold the upper right edge of the small triangular flap to the vertical edge.

5 Swing the left-hand flap to the right, taking all layers with it.

6 Fold the small corner over at right angles, crease firmly, and unfold the flap back to step 3.

7 Now the assembly begins. Lift and squash the flap using existing creases.

8 Swing the lower flap behind to the right. Fold the lower edges of the diamond-shaped flap to the center, crease, and unfold.

9 Lift up the right half of the diamond-shaped flap and make a small reverse fold as you fold it back. Turn the paper over.

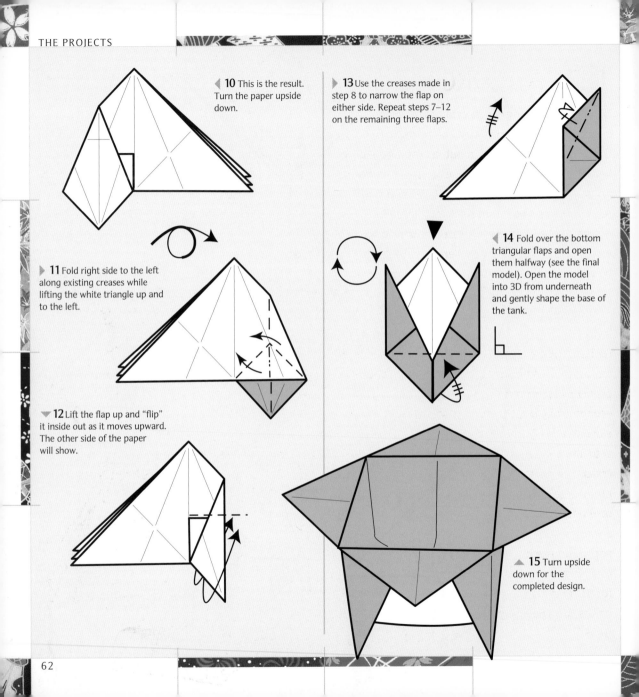

10 This is the result. Turn the paper upside down.

11 Fold right side to the left along existing creases while lifting the white triangle up and to the left.

12 Lift the flap up and "flip" it inside out as it moves upward. The other side of the paper will show.

13 Use the creases made in step 8 to narrow the flap on either side. Repeat steps 7–12 on the remaining three flaps.

14 Fold over the bottom triangular flaps and open them halfway (see the final model). Open the model into 3D from underneath and gently shape the base of the tank.

15 Turn upside down for the completed design.

TETRAHEDRON

Geometric solids hold a fascination for many origami designers. It may well be due to the fact that origami design is all about angles, or possibly because we enjoy seeing shapes in paper and there are few shapes as beautiful as regular and semi-regular solids. You might think that trying to design a cube or (as in this case) a tetrahedron would be an uninspiring challenge, but the aim here is not only to create the shape but to do so using an elegant or unusual method.

Tung Ken Lam, the designer of this model, loves to work with geometric and modular designs. He has the rare ability to surprise and delight with his designs. This model is a classic simply awaiting proper exposure—it uses the paper so economically and the result is so elegant—the finished unit actually requires only five creases. If you want to produce this cleaner result, fold step 1 on a spare sheet of paper and use it as a template for the two halves you need to fold.

1 Start with a square creased in half both ways, colored side upward. Fold the horizontal corners to touch the nearest quarter crease, starting the crease at the vertical corners.

2 This is the result. Turn the paper over.

3 Fold in half from side to side, crease, and unfold.

4 Repeat step 1 on this side—the corners meet the vertical crease.

5 Open the last creases out a little and fold the model a bit more than in half. You can now join the two halves—the two sharper corners slide into matching pockets on the other unit.

6 When you have all four corners tucked in, tighten the model, and it will stay together securely.

63

FOLLOWING UP YOUR INTEREST

When you have worked your way through this book, you may well want to know how to continue your hobby. The answer is simple: fold as many new designs as you can find. Try your local library, search the Internet, and visit your local bookstore (remaindered stores often have an origami title in stock). As well as folding on your own, try to find other people who share your interest—it's a great feeling to fold in a small (or even a large) group.

If you're serious, search out an origami society. There are many of these, all around the world, each with its own magazine full of new designs, photographs, and news. Most have a convention every year, where you can combine a short vacation with some serious folding time!

As well as thousands of origami diagrams, you can find details of origami societies on the Internet. Here are some good places to start:

www.origami-usa.org

www.origami.vancouver.bc.ca

www.paperfolder.info (the author's website)

www.britishorigami.info

CREDITS

All illustrations and photographs are the copyright of Quarto Publishing plc.

AUTHOR'S ACKNOWLEDGEMENTS

I'd like to thank all those at Quarto involved in making this book happen: Moira Clinch, Kate Kirby, Penny Cobb, Jackie Palmer, Karin Skånberg, and Mary Groom. Also to my family: Alison, Daisy, Nick, Matilda, and Gomez Robinson. An extended family certainly prevents any delusions of grandeur. I have made many origami friends over the years, but I owe special thanks to Dave Brill, Paulo Mulatinho, Edwin Corrie (who also proofed these diagrams), Kuni Kasahara, Bob Neale, the late Philip Shen, Mark Kennedy, Gay Gross, Wayne "Grandad" Brown, Mick Guy (and the rest of the BOS council).

Other tipping of the hat to my fellow band members Bev, Steve, John, and Chris (alias the Betty Black band), and to David Mead—long overdue some proper recognition. Anyone due for thanks that I've forgotten, please bear in mind the ravages of time on the human brain.